ANCIENT
ROME

Peter Chrisp

Hello, I'm Flavia

Come and explore
MY WORLD and
find out what it is
like to be a Roman.

My name is Titus

I'm called
Felix

World Book

in association with

W C N

Portage Public Library
2665 Irving Street
Portage, IN 46368

First published in the United States and Canada by
World Book Inc.
525 W. Monroe
Chicago, IL 60661
in association with Two-Can Publishing Ltd.

**For information on other World Book products, call 1-800-255-1750, x 2238,
or visit us at our Web site at http://www.worldbook.com**

Editor: Claire Watts
Art direction and design: Helen McDonagh
Cover design: Helen Holmes
Text: Peter Chrisp
Consultant: Simon James BSc, PhD, The British Museum, London
Senior Managing Editor: Christine Morley
Managing Art Director: Carole Orbell
Model maker: Melanie Williams
Illustrator: David Hitch
Photography: John Englefield
Special thanks to: Melissa Tucker, World Book Publishing

Library of Congress Cataloging-in-Publication Data
Chrisp, Peter.
   Ancient Rome / Peter Chrisp.
     p. cm. — (My world)
   Includes index.
   Summary: While telling about her life in ancient Rome, eight-year
-old Flavia includes information about the homes, families,
clothing, food, gods, sports, goods traded, and things the people
build.
   ISBN 0-7166-9400-X (hbk.) — ISBN 0-7166-9401-8 (pbk.)
   1. Rome—Civilization—Juvenile literature. [1. Rome-
-Civilization.] I. Title. I. Series: My world (Chicago, Ill.)
DG77.C477 1997
937'.6—dc21   97-1364

Printed in Hong Kong

1 2 3 4 5 6 7 8 9 10 01 00 99 98 97

CONTENTS

My name is Flavia. I'm eight years old and I live in Rome, the capital of the Roman Empire. You can see from the map that our empire is very big. It is made up of lots of different lands, but they're all ruled by Romans. Our ruler is a great man called Emperor Trajan.

This map shows the Roman Empire in the 19th year of Emperor Trajan's rule (A.D. 117).

The Roman Empire

Many years ago, Rome was just a small place. Over the past 400 years, our army has conquered many lands and made them into an empire. The Roman Empire is divided into areas called provinces, which are all ruled over by our emperor. Sometimes, people in our empire rebel against Roman rule, but our soldiers are so well trained that nobody can beat them.

The dotted lines show the borders between provinces.

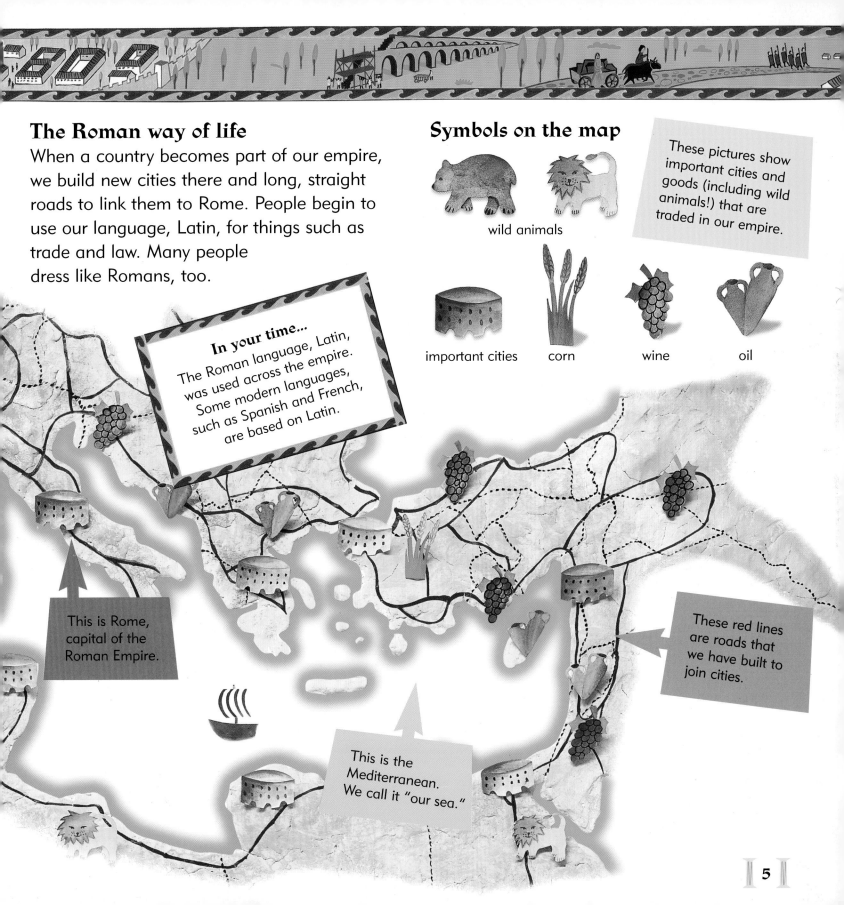

The Roman way of life

When a country becomes part of our empire, we build new cities there and long, straight roads to link them to Rome. People begin to use our language, Latin, for things such as trade and law. Many people dress like Romans, too.

Symbols on the map

These pictures show important cities and goods (including wild animals!) that are traded in our empire.

wild animals

important cities   corn   wine   oil

In your time...
The Roman language, Latin, was used across the empire. Some modern languages, such as Spanish and French, are based on Latin.

This is Rome, capital of the Roman Empire.

These red lines are roads that we have built to join cities.

This is the Mediterranean. We call it "our sea."

I live with my mother and father and my brother Titus, who is ten. Mother is teaching me how to run a home and how to spin wool into thread. But I'd much rather play knucklebones with Titus! It's my favorite game.

I pull the wool into a long thread and use a tool called a spindle to twist it.

Father and Mother

My father has an important job. He's called a senator and he advises the emperor. I don't see Father much, because he's often away traveling on business for the emperor, or visiting our farms in the provinces. My mother stays at home with Titus and me. Every day she has to buy supplies, organize the cooking and cleaning, and give orders to our servants.

Let's make knucklebone toys

Find self-hardening clay, paints, and paintbrush.

1 Mold the clay into 10 knucklebone shapes like these. Let the clay dry.

2 Paint the shapes gray and yellow, then flick brown paint on them, so that they look like bones. Let them dry.

3 Now you are ready to play. Give 5 knucklebones to each player. Take turns throwing the knucklebones up in the air and catching them on the back of your hand. Whoever catches the most is the winner.

A boy's life

My brother, Titus, doesn't have to learn about looking after a home like I do. When he grows up, he will be a lawyer, or a politician, or a soldier – or perhaps all three! This means Titus has to study hard, and Father always asks his tutor how well he is doing. If Titus has misbehaved, Father is very angry!

Roman slaves

We have people called slaves to do the work in our house. You can buy slaves in the market. Some are prisoners who have been captured in a war. Our friend Felix was born a slave, because his parents are slaves. When Felix was younger, he played a lot with Titus and me. Now, he works in our kitchen, but he still plays with us in his free time.

Titus is playing knucklebones with our friend, Felix.

Knucklebones are made from the anklebones of sheep.

Our house is in the center of Rome. It has many grand rooms decorated with wall paintings and floor mosaics, which are pictures made from tiny bits of colored tile and glass. There is a scary mosaic just inside our front door. It shows a fierce dog with the words "Beware of the dog" written above it.

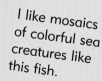

I like mosaics of colorful sea creatures like this fish.

Let's make a mosaic

Find thick cardboard, pencil, colored paper, scissors and glue.

1 Draw the outline of your design onto the cardboard.

2 Decide which color you are going to use for each part of your mosaic and then cut the colored paper into small squares. It doesn't matter if they're a bit uneven.

3 Starting in one corner, spread glue over the cardboard and stick down the colored paper squares to fill in your design.

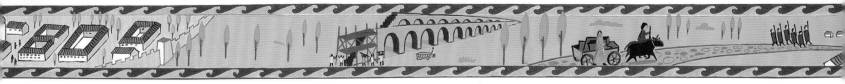

Letting in the light

The biggest room in our house is the entrance hall, called the atrium. It has an opening in the roof, so it's more like a courtyard than a room. The opening lets in lots of light, as well as rainwater, which collects in a pool underneath. We use the water for washing and cooking.

A tour of our house

All around the atrium there are doors and windows leading to other rooms. The kitchen and dining room are on one side, and Father's office is on the other. Some of the bedrooms are downstairs and some are upstairs.

This is my house. The garden has a shady, roofed area where I play.

This is the atrium. Guests wait here when they come to visit my father.

Father rents a room at the front to a shopkeeper who sells cloth.

The dining room has couches for people to lie on when they eat.

Rome is a noisy city, with narrow streets jammed with people rushing here and there. Titus and I aren't allowed out in the crowded streets on our own, so we ask Felix to buy things for us when he goes shopping.

Felix is going to buy wine to fill these big jars, called amphorae.

I'm asking Felix to buy some seed at the market for my pet bird.

Roman coins

The coins I'm handing Felix look like these. The same coins are used in most of our empire.

Every coin has a picture of our emperor on it.

In your time...
Roman coins showed the face of a ruler on one side, just like many coins used today.

The forum

In the middle of the city there's an open area called the forum. People meet here to chat and gossip and to visit the market. Near the forum, there are important public buildings, such as the law courts and temples.

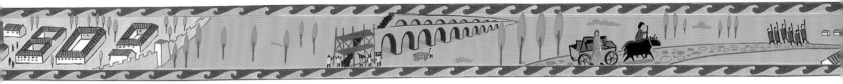

City streets

The streets of Rome run in straight lines and cross each other, dividing the city into lots of blocks, which we call insulae. Insulae are packed with shops, workshops, taverns, and apartments.

Dangerous homes

In Rome, only rich people live in houses like ours. Most people live in small apartments above shops, or in buildings up to five or six floors high. It can be dangerous to live in these apartments, because fires often start and sometimes people can't escape.

This is a section of insulae. Homes and shops are all crowded together.

Families live above shops in one-room apartments.

People collect water from a fountain in the street.

Stepping stones make it easy to cross the road, even when it's raining.

It is warm here for most of the year, so all Romans wear a simple tunic tied at the waist. Our legs are bare and we wear sandals on our feet. Most women wear rings, necklaces, and bracelets, too. On festival days, such as the Floralia, we put on our best tunics and wear garlands of flowers.

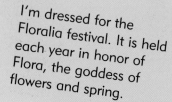

I'm dressed for the Floralia festival. It is held each year in honor of Flora, the goddess of flowers and spring.

Let's make a snake bracelet

Find thin cardboard, scissors, gold, pink, green, and blue paint, paintbrush, thin wire, and tape.

1 Cut the cardboard into the shape of a snake, as shown below.

2 Paint the snake gold. When it's dry, paint on a snakeskin pattern. Now let the snake dry.

Women's clothes

On top of her tunic, Mother wears a long colored robe. If it's a cold day, she wears a thick woolen cloak. She spends a long time getting dressed in the morning. Sometimes she needs three slaves to help her put on her jewelry, perfume, makeup, and wig!

The toga

My father wears a toga on top of his tunic. A toga is a heavy woolen sheet draped in folds around the body. Father hates wearing his toga, because it's very uncomfortable, especially in hot weather. But all important Roman men are supposed to wear togas in public. Even my brother Titus wears a toga on special occasions.

Titus wears a boy's toga with a purple band. When he's 15, he will wear a man's plain white toga.

3 Tape a piece of wire along the back of the snake. Tape over the ends of the wire, too. Now bend the snake around your arm.

Snakes are lucky animals. I wear this bracelet to protect myself from bad luck.

The food we eat

My family is well off, so we can eat and drink delicious things from all over the empire. But most Romans eat the same type of food every day – a stew made from wheat, lentils, or beans. People who are very poor live on porridge made of ground wheat mixed with water.

In these pots we keep honey, pepper, and spicy fish sauce to flavor our food.

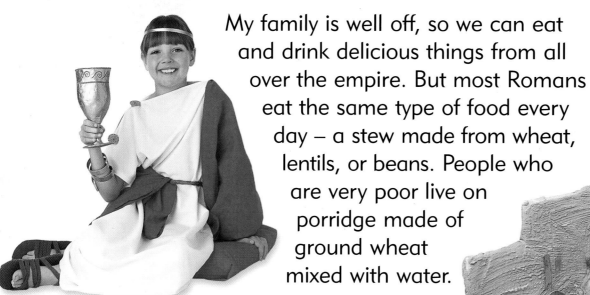

This is the kitchen at our house in Rome. Most Romans don't have a kitchen. They have to buy cooked food from a shop or a tavern.

Our cook

We have a cook called Lucius who works in the kitchen. He makes all our meals and bakes bread each morning in a charcoal oven. Lucius is always busy, especially when Father is at home. Then we have guests for dinner almost every night.

These amphorae are full of olive oil and wine.

Dormice and snails

Sometimes, for a special treat, we have roast dormice. Lucius keeps the dormice in a jar in the kitchen, fattening them up on nuts. He keeps snails too, feeding them milk until they are too fat to get back in their shells. Then he fries them in olive oil and serves them with fish sauce. They taste delicious!

Our gardener sends us fruit from our house in the country.

These sacks are full of flour for making bread.

Let's make grape punch

Adult help needed

Find 2 dates, knife, 1 quart (1 liter) of white grape juice, 4 tablespoons of honey, crushed bay leaf, pinch each of cinnamon, ground pepper, and saffron (optional), wooden spoon, saucepan, lemon slices.

1 Remove the seeds from the dates and ask an adult to chop the dates finely.

2 Put all the ingredients except the lemon in a saucepan. Ask an adult to stir them over a low heat for half an hour.

3 Leave the punch to cool and then pour it into a jug. Decorate with lemon slices and serve.

Titus and I don't have to go to school. Instead, we're taught at home by our Greek slave, Theo. We learn reading, writing, and arithmetic. We practice writing by scratching letters on a wax tablet with a sharp piece of metal called a stylus.

My mother is teaching me to play music on my lyre. It's much more fun than arithmetic!

Let's make a writing tablet and stylus

Find modeling clay, thick cardboard, rolling pin, piece of dowel the same size as a pencil, pencil sharpener, and gold paint.

1 For the writing tablet, put a large piece of clay in the center of the cardboard and roll it into a flat sheet.

2 For the stylus, sharpen the dowel with a pencil sharpener. Paint it gold and let it dry.

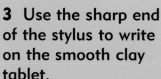

3 Use the sharp end of the stylus to write on the smooth clay tablet.

4 When you have finished, smooth the clay over with your finger and start again.

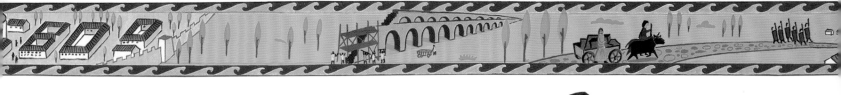

Lessons for boys

When Titus grows up, he might be a politician, so he's learning to make speeches. He has to speak clearly and know how to say difficult words. Theo is teaching Titus Greek as well as Latin. Father says Greek slaves make good teachers because they have usually studied more than their masters!

Titus is reading Greek words written on his writing tablet.

We use letters for writing numbers. These are the numbers one to eighteen.

In your time...
Roman numbers are sometimes used today. Look out for them on clock faces and on buildings and statues.

Going to school

Some of our friends have to go to school. Their parents pay to send them there, but it's not as expensive as having a tutor at home. The teacher beats them if they make mistakes. Theo would never beat us.

Many Roman children don't go to school at all. They find out what they need to know by watching grown-ups work and by helping them. Our slave, Felix, is learning how to cook by helping Lucius in the kitchen.

There's always lots to do in Rome. Many people go to the bathhouse every afternoon. It doesn't cost much and children get in free. Sometimes Titus and I are allowed to go to the theater. The actors wear painted masks and play drums, pipes, and trumpets.

Going to the theater

The theater is very exciting. You can see amazing special effects, with actors swooping across the stage or disappearing through trapdoors in a puff of smoke. The audience always cheers loudly when this happens!

Actors wear masks to show the audience which character they're playing.

On stage, actors beat drums like this with the palms of their hands or their knuckles.

Let's make a drum

Find 2 cardboard strips 2½ in. x 36 in. (6 cm x 90 cm), tape, glue, circle of calico 13 in. (32 cm) in diameter, string, paint, paintbrush, yarn.

1 Tape the ends of one of the strips of cardboard together to make a circle.

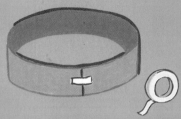

2 Spread glue around the top outside edge of the circle. Stretch the fabric over the circle and hold in place with string until the glue is dry.

3 Take off the string, then spread glue on one side of the other length of cardboard. Wrap it around the drum. Hold it in place with string until the glue is dry.

4 Decorate your drum with paint. Then glue on tassels made from yarn.

Our toys

When we were little, Titus and I played with pull-along animals carved from wood. Now, we have balls, tops, marbles, and pottery dolls with moving arms and legs. Titus has his own little chariot pulled by a pet goat. He loves having races with his friends.

Bathhouses

Most houses don't have bathrooms, so people go to the bathhouse to wash. You can go there to relax and to exercise, too. People wrestle and play ball games, or amuse themselves quietly by playing dice.

Hot air from a furnace travels under the floor to heat the bathhouse.

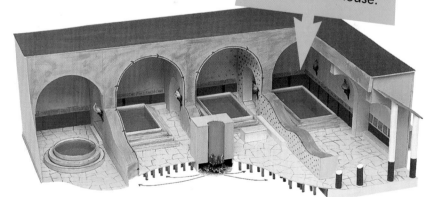

In your time...
The Romans invented central heating. Buildings today are heated in a similar way, often with hot water pipes instead of hot air.

On special days of the year, the emperor puts on free shows, such as chariot races or fights between men called gladiators. Titus and I are too young to go, but we love playing as charioteers and gladiators.

At the circus

Chariot races are the most popular sport in Rome. They take place at a race track called the circus. The charioteers belong to different teams, each with its own color. My parents support the Blues. They're my favorites, too.

Titus and I have model chariots to play with.

Gladiator fights are held here in the amphitheater.

The amphitheater

In most Roman cities, there's a huge building called an amphitheater. The one here in Rome holds thousands of people. Everyone goes to the amphitheater to watch different kinds of contests. You can see prisoners fighting against wild animals, such as leopards and lions, or animals fighting each other.

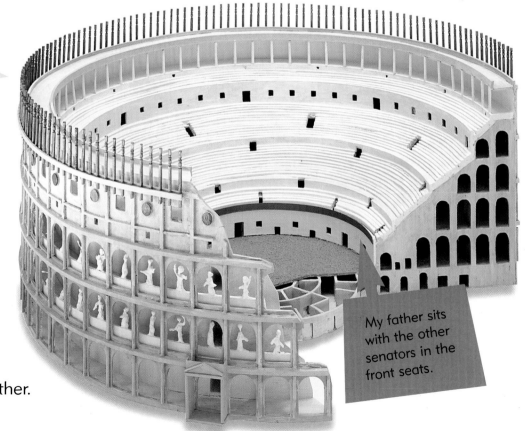

My father sits with the other senators in the front seats.

Brave gladiators

Gladiators are men trained to fight in the amphitheater. They are slaves, but if they are brave and the crowd likes them, the emperor may give them their freedom. Gladiators have fans who cheer them on and watch all their fights. Fans even write the names of the best gladiators on walls!

Antonius wins the pretend fight. He still has his weapon, but Titus has lost his sword.

Titus holds up his finger to show he's surrendering.

A net like this is a useful weapon. If Antonius can throw the net over Titus, Titus can't fight back.

Titus is playing gladiators with his friend Antonius.

Every day, I leave a gift for the gods at a special place in our house called a shrine. We believe in many gods, and they will only help us if we pray to them and bring them gifts. If we are sick, we offer healing charms to help us get better.

Let's make a charm

★ Adult help needed

Find thin cardboard 6 in. x 3 in. (15 cm x 7 cm), pencil, scissors, paintbrush, bronze and gold paint, thumbtack, wire, and gold string.

1 Draw a hand shape and a "candy" shape on the cardboard, and cut them out.

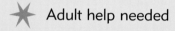

Father is going on a journey today, so I'm leaving flowers at our shrine to ask the gods to keep him safe.

Watching over us

There are different gods to watch over every part of our lives. The most important god is called Jupiter. He protects Rome and our empire. His wife Juno looks after mothers and babies.

Gifts and festivals

Throughout the year, all the gods and goddesses have their own special festivals with ceremonies or processions with music and dancing. If we need help from a particular god or goddess, we visit their temple. Sometimes, the offerings we make are burnt, and the rising smoke carries the gift to the god.

Musicians play at important religious occasions, such as processions and funerals.

2 Paint the shapes, then let them dry. Ask an adult to write your name on the candy shape by making holes with the thumbtack.

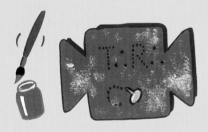

3 Coil the wire into 3 rings and attach the pieces together as shown. Tie gold string to the top ring, so that you can hang your charm.

When my mother hurt her hand, she hung this charm at the temple of Aesculapius, who is the god of healing.

In your time...
The planets Mercury, Venus, Mars, Jupiter, Saturn, and Neptune are all named after Roman gods.

My father has just come back from Dacia, a province that Emperor Trajan conquered before I was born. Father was in charge of setting up new cities and building roads to link them together. As well as lots of new buildings, some cities have a special channel called an aqueduct to carry water into the city.

Aqueducts

It is very important to have a water supply in a city, so that we can keep clean and healthy. If there is no water near a city, an aqueduct is built from the nearest river or lake. Sometimes the water travels a long way before it reaches the city. Most of the time, the aqueduct is underground, but in some places the water travels high above the ground.

Felix brings me water to wash in. It is piped to our house from an aqueduct.

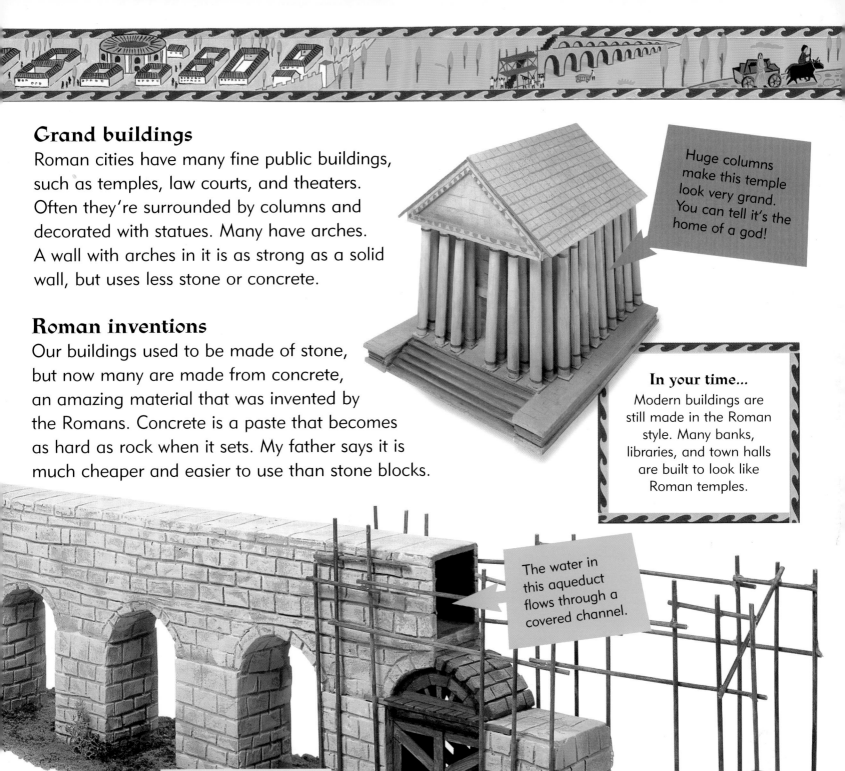

Grand buildings

Roman cities have many fine public buildings, such as temples, law courts, and theaters. Often they're surrounded by columns and decorated with statues. Many have arches. A wall with arches in it is as strong as a solid wall, but uses less stone or concrete.

Roman inventions

Our buildings used to be made of stone, but now many are made from concrete, an amazing material that was invented by the Romans. Concrete is a paste that becomes as hard as rock when it sets. My father says it is much cheaper and easier to use than stone blocks.

Huge columns make this temple look very grand. You can tell it's the home of a god!

In your time...
Modern buildings are still made in the Roman style. Many banks, libraries, and town halls are built to look like Roman temples.

The water in this aqueduct flows through a covered channel.

Arches are built over a wooden frame, which is removed when the arch is complete.

Defending our empire

Sometimes, when our army has won a war, the soldiers march through the streets, leading their prisoners.
Everyone comes out to cheer the soldiers. The most important soldiers and senators wear laurel wreaths, like the one I'm holding.

My father wore a laurel wreath the last time the army marched through Rome.

Protecting our borders

Outside our empire, there are fierce peoples who would like to attack us. We call them barbarians. To protect us, the army builds forts and camps all along the borders of the empire. The soldiers aren't always fighting, though. They build roads and bridges, and carry letters, too.

Let's make a laurel wreath

Find thin cardboard; scissors; light green, dark green, and red paper; paintbrush; paint; glue; and hairpins.

1 Cut out the circular shape shown here from cardboard. Make sure it fits your head.

2 Cut out leaf shapes from green paper. Paint them to look like leaves.

3 When the leaves are dry, glue them onto the wreath.

back

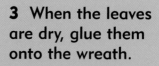

4 Cut a strip of red paper and cut a V in each end. Fold the strip around the back of the wreath and glue it in place. Use hairpins to hold the wreath on your head.

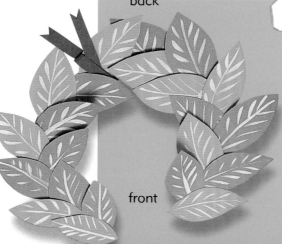

front

Titus's friends are dressed up like soldiers.

A centurion is in charge of 80 soldiers.

The Roman army

Most of our soldiers fight on foot using swords and spears. They are helped by soldiers who fight in other ways. There are cavalrymen from Africa who fight on horseback, and archers from a province called Syria who use bows and arrows.

A centurion's armor is made of shiny metal scales.

Metal greaves, or shin guards, protect the legs.

Syrian archers wear long robes and carry spare arrows on their backs.

The goods we trade

Here in Rome, merchants sell things from all over the empire and beyond. This beautiful silk has come all the way from China. Some goods travel to Rome on carts pulled by mules or oxen, but it's quicker and easier to send things across the sea by ship.

Food and spices

Most of the bread we eat is made from wheat grown in Egypt. The best olive oil comes from Spain and Greece, and my mother's perfume comes all the way across the sea from Arabia. Our cook's spices travel even farther. They come from India and islands farther east. The Mediterranean Sea is busy with Roman merchant ships carrying goods all over the empire.

My mother is going to have a new robe made out of this Chinese silk.

This is a merchant ship. It can carry a huge cargo, but it is very slow.

The wind fills this square sail and pushes the ship along.

Before merchants sell their goods, they weigh them on scales like these.

The cargo is stored inside the deep, wide hold.

The busy harbor

Sometimes, Father takes me to the harbor at Ostia. You can see many ships being unloaded. Some goods are put onto barges and towed up the river to Rome, where they are sold to merchants and shopkeepers.

Theo, our Greek tutor, has been telling us a strange story. He says that once, in North Africa, there was a slave called Androcles. He belonged to a cruel Roman farmer who often beat his slaves. This is what happened to Androcles.

Making an escape

One day, Androcles decided to run away from his cruel master. He fled to the hills and found a cave to hide in.

Before long, Androcles saw a huge shape blocking the entrance to the cave. It was a lion – and it was staring straight at him! Androcles was terrified. He was sure that the lion was going to pounce on him.

But to his surprise, the lion just whimpered and held out his paw. Androcles slowly edged closer, until he could see a large thorn sticking out of the lion's paw. Androcles tugged at the thorn and at last it came out. The lion licked Androcles's face with his rough tongue to say thank you.

From then on, Androcles and the lion were the best of friends. For three years, they lived together in the cave, and every few days the lion went out hunting and brought back meat for both of them to eat. Then one day, Androcles realized he missed people very much, and so he decided to leave the cave.

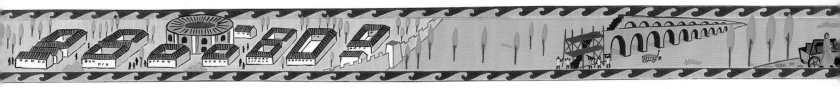

Taken prisoner

Unfortunately, Androcles hadn't got very far before he was captured by some Roman soldiers. They arrested Androcles and sent him to Rome, where the emperor was looking for new prisoners to fight in one of his shows.

The fiercest lion

Many months later, Androcles found himself standing in the huge amphitheater in Rome. The crowd clapped and cheered as several snarling lions were led into the arena.

Androcles trembled with fear as the biggest lion ran toward him. But right at the last moment the lion suddenly stopped. Instead of attacking Androcles, the lion gently licked his feet. Androcles recognized the beast as his friend from the cave.

The emperor couldn't believe his eyes. He accused the animal handlers of sending a tame lion into the ring. The animal handlers said the lion was one of the fiercest they'd ever seen. So the emperor sent for Androcles to ask him why the lion wouldn't fight him.

The emperor's decision

Androcles explained how he and the lion had once lived together in the cave. The emperor knew there was only one thing he could do now and, with a cheer from the crowd, he freed Androcles and the lion.

And from that day on, people became quite used to the sight of Androcles leading his lion friend through the streets of Rome.

Clues they left

Flavia's world

Flavia lived nearly 2,000 years ago, but today we know many things about that time. People who study the past, called archaeologists, can piece together the story of ancient Rome from clues that the Romans left behind.

Roman writings

Archaeologists have found books and papers written by the Romans. As well as books about history and religion, there are stories, cook books, and letters.

Ancient buildings

There are many Roman buildings, such as aqueducts, temples, and amphitheaters, still standing all over the lands that were once part of the Roman Empire. In southern Italy, archaeologists have dug up a whole Roman city, called Pompeii, which was buried in ash and mud when a volcano erupted.

The huge amphitheater where gladiators fought still stands in Rome.

Index

The words in bold are things for you to make.